FUNNY FAITH

*I'm Convinced God is Somewhere
Laughing at Me*

Sam L. Townsend, Jr.

FUNNY FAITH
I'm Convinced God is Somewhere Laughing at Me

Copyright © 2016 by Sam L. Townsend, Jr.
All Rights Reserved.

No part of this book may be used or reproduced, stored in retrieval system or transmitted in any form or by any means – electronic, mechanical, photocopying, recording or otherwise – without the written permission of Sam L. Townsend, Jr. and RiverHouse Publishing, LLC

Scripture quotations marked NIV are taken from the New International Version of *The Holy Bible*.

Song Lyric quotation of "Hold to God's Unchanging Hand" is in the public domain.

This book is dedicated to (*state your name*).

Acknowledgments

The completion of this book could not have been accomplished without the persistent nudging of my friend and brother, Kenneth Taylor and Kingmaker Strategies. What began as a far-fetched text message between two friends has turned into something I am very proud of. *High-five!

To Reverend Dr. Leslie Braxton and the New Beginnings Christian Fellowship, thank you for giving me a place to reinvent myself and for inspiring me to dream and achieve. Also to our Poet Laureate, Dr. Mona Lake Jones who gave me one of the greatest endorsements by calling me "a fellow author." Thank you for helping me end my love affair with commas.

To my son, my siblings and my parents, thanks for being a never-ending supply of love and laughter. I'm really blessed to be in a family of superheroes.

Finally, to God... I'd love to have your autograph.

Table of Contents

Introduction 1
Chapter 1 - Who Am I? 4
Chapter 2 - Good Morning 9
Chapter 3 - "An Orange Valencia" 15
Chapter 4 - Grow in Grace 20
Chapter 5 - Home Improvements 24
Chapter 6 - Minister, Meet Yourself 28
Chapter 7 - I Declare War 33
Chapter 8 - The Little Black Book 38
Chapter 9 - You Look A Mess 47
Chapter 10 - Church Boy 54
Chapter 11 –My Son is Driving Me Nuts 65
Chapter 12 - Decisions, Decisions 72

Introduction

If God were to allow us to read the pages of our lives in advance, chances are we couldn't handle the story and would probably refuse to ever have it published. We would become fearful of the chapters full of battles, paralyzed by the exclamation marks of pain, addicted to the joys in the footnotes, distracted by the index of failures and confused by the countless lines of silence - where God said and wrote nothing. So instead, The Great Author of time wrote one line on a small bookmark, "All things work for your good" and left these instructions: "Place on every page necessary." He personally signed the bookmark "Intentional."

Looking back over my life I can see so many pages where I really needed to use that bookmark. There were so many times I needed to be reminded that even though I make mistakes, whatever God does with those mistakes is intentional. Every turn of events, good or bad, will work in my favor. Without really understanding how God helps us write our story, in the moment I missed some of the most life transforming lessons. These lessons were hidden in what seemed like insignificant experiences and sometimes unfortunate circumstances. This is why I wrote, *Funny Faith – I'm Convinced God is Somewhere Laughing at Me*. I wrote this book to share with you some examples of how God teaches us about ourselves, about Him and the lessons that I've learned about myself. These are lessons that God has probably been trying to teach you too, you just didn't realize it at the time.

When God laughs at us, it's not in a cruel sense. It's more like a father taking joy in the fact that his child trusts him so completely that he would take a leap of faith. Throughout my life I've seen my Heavenly Father with His arms outstretched saying, "Sam, jump!" Then I can hear Him giggling a little as I fall into his arms, abandoning all fear and hesitation. When I'm feeling awkward about a decision I've made or am about to make, I have a nervous laugh. I think God has a type of nervous laugh too when He sees some of the decisions we've made. I've also seen Him teach me the greatest lessons through those odd and awkward circumstances. Then there's the somewhat passive aggressive laugh we make when something is going wrong or someone is acting like a fool, but you laugh to keep from going off. God's got that laugh too. This book was written for those of you who are on the verge of taking that leap of faith. It's also for those who feel like you're sinking in the sands of your own procrastination. It's for those who can't seem to get over the wall that is blocking their path to destiny. It's also to encourage those who are walking the road of divine purpose. It's for parents needing help raising their children and for children struggling to understand their over protective parents. This book is for those who have become disenchanted with the church and for those ready to start a new work. It's a book to remind you of God's patience, grace and humor, as well as His discipline and expectations of us as His children. It's for anyone who needs to know that they are not alone in life or in ministry. *Funny Faith* is my collection of personal humorous oddities, everyday moments, precious memories and biblical truths that God has used to reveal His glory and purpose in my life. It is my prayer that as you read this book, you will begin to listen and hear the laughter of the Father around you and embrace the joy of the Lord, which is our strength.

Chapter 1 - Who Am I?

When you are young in age or in your Christian walk it can be difficult to really understand who you are in God's plan. Growing up, I had no idea who I was. I knew I was the first born of my parents. My dad was a Seattle Police Officer turned pastor and my mom was a devout Catholic girl turned Pentecostal evangelist. I knew I was their son and to me that was the sum of my identity. I also knew I was a church boy, a choir boy to be more specific and that identity seemed to work against me in my adolescent years. I was always teased in middle school. I had very light skin and often thought to be Caucasian. I had bad acne, big lips, low self-esteem and to top it all off, I was a church boy. As a defense mechanism, I learned to laugh and make fun of myself before anyone else could. The way I figured it, making fun of myself hurt much less than getting beat up and bullied. I began to find the humor in every personal embarrassment, insecurity and awkward situation. I made the kids laugh with me before they could laugh at me. For example, in our house the only music we could listen to was church music. You could always here Andrae Crouch, the Clark Sisters or the Hawkins coming from our record player. So when I got to school and all the kids were singing and dancing to the latest R&B tunes, I looked like the odd ball. When the kids would ask what kind of music I listened to, I would reply,

"Country Western." I figured I could easily make up titles and lyrics and none of them would be the wiser. I guess at the time, pretending that I was a cowboy seemed easier than explaining that I was a church boy.

As I entered high school I became known as the class clown. At least that was the side of me that I allowed my classmates to see. When no one was around, I was still the lonely teenager who ate lunch alone sitting on the merry-go-round at the playground next to my high school. What made it worse was that when the kids from the daycare would come out and play, I was on their turf. I got kicked off the playground by pre-preschoolers! I felt like I just didn't belong anywhere. But I learned early on to make the best out of bad situations. Over the next few years I graduated high school, started working, got engaged, got married, started a family, had a son and later sadly got a divorce. Once again, I felt like I just didn't belong, not even in my own life. In that 7-year span of time I made a lot of mistakes, but one thing my dad taught me was that there is life after stupid. At the age of 26 I started my own music ministry, the Imani Fellowship Choir. It was with this group of singers and musicians that I began to rebuild my self-esteem. I began to recognize my worth to others around me and explore my greatest passion, music. I started taking the simple songs that I had written as a teenager while directing the youth choir, updated them and taught them to Imani. I eventually recorded them. I wasn't classically trained and couldn't read music. I taught myself to play the piano, which was something I never thought would be possible. You see the church where both my parents accepted Christ was called Tolliver Temple Church of God in Christ. This was one of the very popular Pentecostal churches in the 1970's, with a very strong music ministry. I loved it. As a child I use to watch the organist, Sister Mary Jean McGraw, play that Hammond B3 until the church folk almost danced out of their clothes. I wanted to play like that. So when my dad started pastoring, I remember being about 10 years old on my knees in a prayer revival he was running at our church, Greater Glory Church of God in Christ. My parents taught me how to pray and to pray hard. There I was, on my knees fervently begging God to give me the gift of playing the piano. I wanted our little storefront church that leaned to the side with just a handful of members to have the type of glorious music ministry of the big church we came from. Suddenly I felt something. I lifted my head from the wooden pew and fixed my eyes on the old dusty upright brown piano we had sitting in the corner. While the saints were in a full-on Acts chapter 1, upper room, Holy Ghost fire falling from heaven, prayer experience, I began to stagger down the isle of the little lopsided church. As the legendary Sophia Petrillo of *The Golden Girls* would say, "Picture it!" I was 10 years old with tears in my eyes, a tingling in my fingers, lips quivering, faith in my soul and positioned for a miracle. With my heart pounding to the rhythm of the prayers of the saints I could hear from pews, I began to bang on the piano - and bang, and bang, and bang. What was this horrible sound I was creating? It didn't resemble anything like the gift of music I had asked God for. It wasn't even a joyful noise, it was just noise. What happened to my miracle? Thankfully, the church folks were praying so loud that I don't think they noticed. Silently laughing to myself, I faked like I was in still in the spirit and staggered back to my pew. After that night I decided maybe instead of waiting for a miracle, I'd start practicing and take the time to teach myself to play the piano, which I did. That was the first night I remember thinking that God must be somewhere laughing at me – I know I was.

It took me years to own my identity, to become comfortable in my own skin and to discover my own potential and worth. I had to accept that not everyone would see or be able to understand my purpose. It was more important that above all else, I did. I had to realize that the journey I was on was going to be a lot like the country western songs I pretended to know as a middle school student – full of disappointments and sadness. I really did have a dog that ran away and a parakeet that died of a broken heart. Doesn't that sound just like a country western? I had to come to terms with being skinny, with big lips, non-athletic and a little socially awkward. I never discovered the beauty of music until I decided I would rather make my own noise than live in someone else's silence. I had to declare that I am fearfully and wonderfully made. I am who God designed me to be and I don't need permission to live in that freedom. I am who I am and whatever God desires to change, He will. Until then, each and every day I do my best to live into the greatness I was created to be.

When we were kids, my parents use to buy us ID bracelets with our name, address and phone number engraved on them. I guess the bracelets were in case we got lost, or if someone kidnapped us they would know where to send us back when we got on their nerves. Maybe it's time you invested in a spiritual ID bracelet. Find some scriptures that describe who God says you are and engrave them in your mind. That way if you ever get lost or kidnapped by the enemy, you'll both be reminded of who and whose you are. Trust me, you'll soon get on the devil's nerve and he'll drop you right back off where you belong – in God's Word.

Chapter 2 - Good Morning

I woke up one dreary morning in Seattle with a very fragmented idea cluttering my mind. It was one of those in-between times when you're not all the way asleep but you haven't fully awakened yet either. You know how it is some mornings when you're lying in bed trying to remember a dream but the more you think, the more the dream fades away. I tossed and turned trying to chase my thoughts. The idea that I was wrestling with was, what is the difference between the words *lightened* and *enlightenment*. As intrigued as I was by this early Monday morning philosophical debate with myself, I really just wanted to go back to sleep. I had hoped that if God were speaking in code, His message would become clearer while I rested my eyes. After all, I had worked really hard in ministry on Sunday trying to follow His voice as I led the people in worship. I figured the Lord owed me some extra rest. Suddenly I felt as if God were saying He absolutely owed me nothing. Either I would get up and search this thing out, or it would be lost along with all the other unrevealed and underdeveloped revelations He had given me. There were so many hidden treasures that I missed out on, merely because I decided to sleep. I sat up and the Lord told me to read II Samuel the twelfth chapter. I got out of bed, went into my study and started reading.

"Then Nathan said to David, You are the man! This is what the Lord, the God of Israel, says: 'I anointed you king over Israel, and I delivered you from the hand of Saul. I gave your master's house to you, and your master's wives into your arms. I gave you all Israel and Judah. And if all this had been too little, I would have given you even more. Why did you despise the word of the Lord by doing what is evil in his eyes? You struck down Uriah the Hittite with the sword and took his wife to be your own. You killed him with the sword of the Ammonites. Now, therefore, the sword will never depart from your house, because you despised me and took the wife of Uriah the Hittite to be your own.' "This is what the Lord says: 'Out of your own household I am going to bring calamity on you. Before your very eyes I will take your wives and give them to one who is close to you, and he will sleep with your wives in broad daylight." (II Samuel 12:7-11, NIV). After reading this I thought the Lord must had stopped by the wrong house because I'm not married and I ain't killed nobody. That moment felt like when you're in church and the preacher is preaching heavy on a sin topic and nobody wants to make eye contact with each other. So I just sat in my bed alone, staring at the wall, waiting for the Lord to explain himself.

The Lord began to show me that judgement came because of the disregard David showed for his blessings. God had generously blessed his life. Despite all that God had already given him, David still wanted more. He had Uriah killed and slept with his wife Bathsheba. David and Bathsheba had a son. That son later became sick and died. The prophet Nathan shows up and basically says, "I know what you did and God's going to get you together real quick." Doesn't that sound like it could have been an episode in *Scandal*?

What an eye opening revelation and an opportunity to examine myself. Have I been so blessed and yet negligent of those blessings at the same time? With all the opportunities, gifts, talents and ideas that God has given me, have I become greedy like David? Have I dishonored God by desiring and pursuing what He has not purposed for me? Is there self-pride in my praise? Is my worship really to Him or is it just entertaining my flesh? As a worship leader, preacher and gospel artist, center stage can become very addicting and self-satisfying. No matter how loud the applause is or how great the acclaim, I sometimes still want more. I think most talented singers would be lying if they said they have always only wanted God to get the glory. Oh please! Nobody runs and riffs as much as gospel singers do just to glorify God. Let's be real. God created our voice but we conjure up a lot of the acrobatics that we do with it. I bet God looks at us sometimes shaking his head and shouting, "dismount already!"

While David pondered Nathan's words, calamity struck in the immediate seven days of sickness and subsequent death of David's son. The Bible records that during the first six days, David was completely inconsolable. He was paralyzed in his ability to function as a king over his followers or even as a husband to his wife. He refused to eat or speak with anyone. He stripped himself of his royal garb and for several days he laid on the ground in a coarse black cloth made of goat's hair. He covered himself in ashes as a sign of mourning. The elders of the house remained by his side to help him up from the ground, but he repeatedly refused. However, on the seventh day when he received word that his son had died, David got himself up from the ground. He washed himself, put on lotions, changed his clothes, went into the house of the Lord and worshipped. He then went to his own house, ate a meal, and made love to his wife. David sure knew how to bounce back! But doesn't it make you wonder why there was such a peculiar change in his behavior after such a devastating outcome?

Many times when we are faced with the consequences of our actions we try to find ways to *lighten* the burden on our heart. We do this by making vows and commitments in our mind to do better. We remind ourselves of all the promises of grace and mercy God has given us and then we start cashing in on them like a good payday check. However, I've learned that the most challenging areas of my life required more than a lightened heart and a vow that I'll probably break. Those situations required an *enlightened* response. That is a change not only in your thinking but an evident reform of your actions. True repentance calls for one to put forth effort that results in the fulfillment of the commitments you made in your mind.

While David's son was sick he wanted to believe that the situation would not turn out as severely as it was appearing. No doubt, David began to do as many of us do when facing difficult times, we bargain with God - "Lord, if you do this...then I will do that." It is those promises that temporarily lighten our heart and keep us going. But like David, there comes a time when we must dust off the ashes. Come out of those heavy uncomfortable garments of regret and disappointment and put on garments of praise. Do more than just sit around waiting for your burdens to be lightened. Stand up and become who God has ordained you to be and do what He has empowered you to do.

God is not out to get you. Now He will get you together but it's always for your making not your breaking. God loves you and He only wants the best for you. Don't become comfortable with "one day I will" type of thinking. Newton's First Law of Motion states that "a body at rest will remain at rest unless an outside force acts on it and a body in motion will remain in motion unless acted upon by an outside force." Spiritually speaking, God is that force and perhaps today He's using your current situation to wake you out of your sleep. He's using your situation to set your life back in motion toward your destiny. God never sleeps and the bible only records once since the beginning of time the He even rested. God has been working on your good mornings for as long as He has existed. Now it's time for you to wake up and begin living in them.

For years I made resolutions and commitments to write a book. I was paralyzed by the mistakes of my past. I sat in fear and began to believe the lie that I told myself that I had nothing of value to say. After reading this story about David I laughed because I could hear God saying, "You're going to tell your story or I'm going to." I replied, "No Lord! You're not going to be putting my business in the street like you did David." I quickly picked up a pen and starting writing this book because there's no telling what God will say when He starts talking. I'd rather tell my story my way.

Chapter 3 - "An Orange Valencia"

There's an old hymn that says, "Time is filled with swift transition. Naught of earth unmoved can stand. Build your hope on things eternal. Hold to God's unchanging hand." In order to keep your balance and momentum during a transition, the foundation you stand on must be solid and your faith must be rooted in that foundation. If you are rooted, the winds of your past may bend you but they won't break you. Even when the rain may be pouring down in your present and obscures your view, it does not change the shining bright hope of your promised future. Jeremiah 29:11 say, "For I know the thoughts that I think toward you, says God. Thoughts of good and not of evil, to give you a hope and a future." As a child I believed that at midnight all the street lights everywhere shut off and the world came to a complete stop. I figured it was the law. It wasn't until one night when my father took me fishing around 2:00am that I discovered life keeps going after midnight. This was a powerful revelation of that scripture I carried with me the rest of my life.

In high school I struggled with being accepted by my peers. For example, there was a girl named Michelle that I knew who was the complete opposite of me. She was a cheerleader; I sang in the gospel choir. She was the Vice President of the Black Student Union; I was the switchboard operator in the main office. She was smart; I took geometry twice and not by choice. She was pretty and hip; I wore church shoes to school every day. She was popular; I was unknown. Although we never acknowledged or associated with each other in high school, as fate would have it, we became best friends through a mutual friend years later. She is one of the most intelligent people I know. I can always rely on her to give me good advice whether it's about music business since we're both accomplished gospel artists and ministers, or even advice on raising my son since she has a degree in psychology and human behavior. Yeah she's pretty smart. A few years ago, Michelle received an out-of-state job offer. As excited as I was for her, the closer it came to her departure date, the more I felt at a loss. In a jokingly passive-aggressive manner I started sending her text messages that expressed my extreme distress over her relocation. So dramatic I know. I would make sure that the simplest conversation spiraled into a humorous pit of personal despair. In one text she told me that I spelled a word wrong. I texted back, "Who's gonna correct my spelling when you're gone?" Another day, we made plans to go to breakfast. I texted, "Who am I gonna have scrambled eggs with when you're gone?" On another day, she gave me some advice on dealing with the stress of ministry. I texted back, "Who's gonna talk me off the ledge when you're gone?" Every time her reply was, "It will still be me." Then one afternoon I texted, "Who's gonna teach me to be articulate when you're gone?" Her response was, "He shall not leave you without. Indeed, you shall become." Although I thought her use of the kings English on a non-church day was a bit much, that statement introduced a new reality and a new season in my life.

One of Michelle's favorite summertime beverages is a Venti Orange Valencia with two Splenda. Not being a huge Starbucks connoisseur I decided to experiment and try it out one day. My, my, my it was good! From that time forward I made it a point to enjoy the refreshing beverage about once a week while sitting in a park or driving around the lake. On one particular day I was feeling a little less than productive. There were several personal projects I'd committed to completing in the next six months, but I found myself slowly slipping back into an old habit of procrastination. I remember wishing that everything would just magically happen for me, somehow. I mean, I had some amazing ideas, but bringing them to fruition was a challenge. However, I didn't want to look up a year later and regret that I hadn't taken advantage of the time and resources I had. Looking into the future, I could almost hear Michelle's voice in my head, saying, "Man, you really should have done that."

Feeling compelled to reset the direction of my life, I went to Starbucks to pick up a Venti Orange Valencia...with two Splenda. When I got there, a woman in front of me was paying for her drink. Or at least that's what she was attempting to do. The cashier said, "That will be $5.83," and the woman handed her a gift card. The cashier ran the card, which only had $0.72 on it, and said, "Okay, you need $5.11." The woman reached into her purse and handed the cashier a dollar bill and a fistful of change. Patiently, the cashier counted the money and with a somewhat forced smile, she informed the woman, "You still need $3.27." Without hesitation, the woman began to dig in her purse and pulled out two quarters, a dime and seven pennies. By this time I was thinking I must be on Candid Camera.

Kindly, the cashier counted the coins on the counter, put them in the till, adjusted the amount received so far in the register, directed the woman's attention to the screen by pointing to her balance and said, "You still need $2.60." The woman reached into her purse three more times, each time with more aggression, like she was searching through the very lining. Bit by bit she pulled out pennies, nickels and dimes. When she got down to only needing $0.27 more, being amused but getting impatient, I started to offer to pay it myself. But since the whole situation was so unbelievable, I told myself, "Naw, I'm gonna let her find it herself, right down to the last $0.27." And that's exactly what she did.

When she handed the cashier her last quarter, nickel and two pennies she took her drink and walked away in confidence, as if this entire transaction took place just as it should have. I stepped up and ordered my Venti Orange Valencia with two Splenda, took the cash out of my pocket with ease, paid for my beverage and walked away. Then I realized the woman and I had something in common. What we both needed, we already had. Although I didn't need a gift card and a pound of change to pay my bill, the woman didn't need my help either. I just had to access what I knew I had and she just had to dig a little deeper.

I decided that day that I had to stop asking who was going to help me do and become what God had purposed for me to do and become. He had given me every gift, talent, idea and strategy that I needed to accomplish His purpose. He'd brought me into a new season where if I wanted to realize my dreams, I may to have to dig a little deeper, but what I need is there inside me.

I took my Orange Valencia and drove to the lake. Feeling motivated by what God had just shown me, I parked in a shaded spot by the water, rolled my windows down, opened my sunroof and started writing this chapter. Five minutes later, a bird flew over and crapped on my head through the sunroof. Out loud I said, "Really God! You've got to be joking!"

In a way, I felt like He was saying "Hey, I never said there wouldn't be distractions or setbacks while pursuing your purpose."

Nevertheless, whatever your Venti Orange Valencia dream is, go get it. Stop waiting for a rhema word, a revelation, or a prophetic call. Just do what God has fully equipped you to do. "Being confident of this, that he who began a good work in you will carry it on to completion until the day of Christ Jesus." (Philippians 1:16 NIV)

Chapter 4 - Grow in Grace

I serve as the Minister of Music & Worship Art at New Beginnings Christian Fellowship in Kent, Washington. Anytime I go to rehearse with one of my choirs I usually go with a word from the Lord to share with the choir members. I don't always have time to stop and prepare something, so it has developed into a kind of unspoken agreement and expectation that the Lord and I have. Usually just going about my day something interesting will happen and I'll sense that there's something spiritual in it. Before I know it, the Lord has created an entire sermon out of a simple mishap. For example, on one particular night I was rushing and looking in the mirror on the way out the door I noticed how unshaven my face was.

I'm not someone who'd go to rehearsal all stubbly and I am absolutely against letting my gray hair show...ever. Call me vain - that's fine. But at forty-six years old I like it when people think I'm twenty-six because I age so well. And I know what you're thinking but I already told you in Chapter 2, "my book, my story, my way." All my life I've had very sensitive skin. If I've been drinking too much soda, not drinking enough water or if I've been eating too much chocolate my skin will begin to break out. Bad habits are hard to break. That, coupled with shaving with a straight razor irritates my skin and I sometimes develop ingrown hairs. The best way for me to address this issue is not to shave at all for a few days and to let the hairs grow out. After I've gone through this process, I can shave, my skin is smooth and I look twenty-six again. Go ahead and say it with me, "his book, his story, his way."

When I get dressed I like to do it with purpose. Not always a suit and tie, but not a torn t-shirt and wrinkled jeans either. I like to look put together and appropriately dressed for the task and responsibility of being a leader at all times. I was feeling a bit disheveled on this particular day because although I was dressed appropriately for rehearsal, my face was unshaven. But, I had to let my facial hair grow out if I wanted to address the issues that had developed due to my lack of dietary discipline. Then I heard the Spirit say, "And there are some other things you have to learn to grow out of."

In II Peter 3:18 (NIV), the apostle Peter admonishes us to "grow in the grace and knowledge of our Lord and Savior Jesus Christ." The grace that we grow into is an appreciation for what God has done. The grace of God is undeserved favor. The way we grow into that appreciation of grace and in a deeper understanding of God and His will for our lives is by reading His word and spending time in prayer. It's by actively putting off things that will distract us from fulfilling our purpose. Just like God wants us to grow out of some things, He also wants us to grow into some things. The apostle Paul said that when he was a child, he spoke as a child, but when he got older, he put away childish things. One of my pet peeves is hearing grown people talk in baby voices or act like children.

At some point everyone should hit spiritual puberty. When we are too stubborn to allow the natural process of maturity to occur we become stunted in our growth. We become stunted mentally, spiritually, physically and emotionally. This impairs our ability to function productively in society and spiritually speaking, it limits our ability to live as we should in the Kingdom of God as mature Kingdom citizens. Wouldn't it be funny looking if I came walking down your street in a onesie? The kind with the feet sewn in them. Well, God laughs at you when you keep putting on things you should have grown out of by now. They don't fit! Stop it!

    I hate the rough look of letting my gray facial hair grow and the irritation that comes along with it, drawing undesired attention of others. I don't like people looking at me, wondering why I look like Rip Van Winkle. But as much as I don't like it, the process is necessary. Your growth as a maturing Christian will be unattractive sometimes and it will draw more attention than you desire. You'll find that you won't be able to laugh at inappropriate jokes, because you're growing. Your fasting and prayer life may increase and take time away from socializing with your friends, because you're growing. You may not be spending your fifteen minute breaks at work drinking coffee and gossiping with coworkers, because you're growing. You'll start ignoring phone calls and text messages from friends who want to watch Netflix and chill, because you're growing. Your friends and family may think you're trying to be extra holy, but just keeping growing.

FUNNY FAITH

My dad preached a sermon once titled, "It's painful, but it's necessary." Growth is uncomfortable. It takes you through phases of development that will alter your appearance and not always in the most flattering way. But when it (whatever your *it* is) grows out, that's when God begins to shape it all up. He beautifies the meek with salvation. In Ezekiel 16:6-8 (NIV), the Lord says, "Then I passed by and saw you kicking about in your blood, and as you lay there in your blood I said to you, "Live!" I made you grow like a plant of the field. You grew and developed and entered puberty. Your breasts had formed and your hair had grown, yet you were stark naked. Later I passed by, and when I looked at you and saw that you were old enough for love, I spread the corner of my garment over you and covered your naked body. I gave you my solemn oath and entered into a covenant with you, declares the Sovereign Lord, and you became mine."

Yes, God loves you no matter what, but He will still call out your ugliness for what it is so that you can deal with it honestly and thoroughly. In the process, He'll cover you with grace while you are maturing into what He has predestined you to be. You represent your Creator and what you become and how you reach the point matters to Him. Once you know better, He expects you to do better.

Chapter 5 - Home Improvements

I was lying in bed one cold December night and kept hearing this strange sound. As annoying as it was I refused to emerge from the warmth of my comforter to go investigate. I was all wrapped up like a pig in a blanket so I just rolled over and ignored the sound. The next morning as I was getting ready for work I heard it again. Every five minutes or so I would hear this double chirp from somewhere down the hall. Since I was running late as usual, I didn't have time to worry about it. I mean it was just a chirp right? This went on for several weeks (don't judge me).

After coming home from church one night I noticed that as soon as I walked through my front door my condo seemed strangely warm. Now, I do hate being cold but I don't normally leave my heat on all day. Wasted heat means wasted money. I started walking through my home checking all the thermostats but they were all off. I assumed that the heat from the unit below was rising and warming my place. Well, I wasn't going to complain about that to anybody. The bible says the wealth of the wicked is laid up for the righteous! Laid up – right up to my condo. Thank Ya Lord! This abundance of heat continued happening for about two weeks. I considered it to be a blessing I would just have to live with. Isn't that just like the Lord? Well, that's what I kept telling myself.

FUNNY FAITH

A friend of mine needed to store some extra clothes at my place. Over time, a couple of items turned into several large bags piled up in my living room. I was planning on putting them in the storage closet outside but I didn't want to go out in the cold. You know how I feel about being cold. So the bags remained in my living room for a few days until I decided it was time to do some house cleaning. One evening to get motivated, I turned on some music and grabbed the remote to my electric fireplace. *Click...click*. The fireplace wouldn't turn on. I checked the batteries in the remote but I couldn't tell if they were old or new. I didn't worry about it. After all, the neighbor downstairs was still blessing me with free heat. Thanks, neighbor.

I kept cleaning and the first thing I wanted to do was get those bags out of my living room. Instead of lugging the bags outside in the cold, I decided to move the bags to the spare room and hide them in there. You know, in case I had company. As I started dragging bags down the hall, I could hear, *chirp...chirp.* There was that sound again. I looked up and realized that the chirping was coming from my smoke detector. Apparently, the batteries were dying and the alert was going off to let me know it was time to replace them. Okay, I decided I would change them, later. I know I might sound lazy but maybe you're just reading lazy. It couldn't be me, or could it?

I grabbed the bags of clothing and as I opened the door to the spare room where I was going to hide them, I was hit with a burst of hot air like I was walking into an inferno. "Why is it so hot in here?" I said to myself. It felt like the devil left his front door open. I rechecked the thermostat like I had weeks ago. Although it was still set at zero, when I checked the baseboard I could feel there was heat blowing like I had set the thermostat on ninety-five. Clearly something was wrong. My number one priority was still to get those bags out of plain sight. So I threw them in the overly heated spare room and just shut the door. I walked down the hall ignoring the *chirp...chirp* from the smoke detector, walked into the living room, took the remote to the inoperable fireplace and put it in a drawer in the kitchen. At the end of the night my home looked clean and orderly. However, a closer survey of my home revealed that I still had a cluttered spare room that was hiding bags that didn't belong to me, a dying smoke detector, a malfunctioning fireplace and a thermostat that didn't work. It was at this point that I could imagine God rolling his eyes saying, "You're just going ignore everything aren't you?" This was one of those times when God, being annoyed, laughed at my foolishness.

Sometimes, we treat our Christianity like I treated my home. What if the broken mechanism in the fireplace and the thermostat's faulty wiring had started an actual fire? I wouldn't have been able to depend on the smoke detector because I'd let the batteries die. Too often we ignore the warning of the Holy Spirit that lets us know when our spiritual batteries are low. It's easy to disregard the signs that something is wrong or that there is a deficiency until the consequences hit us in the face like the gust of heat when I walked into my spare room. Instead of

FUNNY FAITH

dealing with inconvenient truths we live in comfortable lies. Instead of increasing our prayer life or investing more time in the Word of God, we create meaningless agendas in an effort to keep up appearances. Our lives can become cluttered with emotional baggage that isn't even ours. Instead of giving it back to whom it belongs or not accepting it in the first place, we shift it from one area of our lives to another. Wow, what if that's why I'm still a bachelor? What if that's why you're still in the situation you're in? God wants us to deal with the *"chirp...chirp"* and the *"click...click"* in our lives before we destroy our own and possibly the other lives that are connected to us.

Well the Lord got my attention. I had the entire heating system in my home replaced. I took the unclaimed bags of clothes to Goodwill. I now change the batteries in my smoke detector regularly. I don't even use the fireplace anymore, after all, it was *fake fire* anyhow. I wonder if God did an inspection of your life, what home improvements would He recommend you make?

Chapter 6 - Minister, Meet Yourself

If you haven't met the person who reminds you of you at your worst, keep living. He or she is coming. Over the course of 2 months or so I started noticing that one of my ministry workers, who is also like a sister to me, was repeatedly making some really poor choices in ministry, her community relations and her interactions with other colleagues. She was also dealing with a lot of disappointment over mistakes she had made and she was thinking of calling it quits. Sometimes it does seem easier to just throw in the towel than to wash the towel and its stains of guilt in Christ's love. We can be so unforgiving of ourselves. I was concerned because I could see myself, my former self in her. I knew the outcome was going to be all bad so I needed to say something. I needed to introduce *her* to the *her* the rest of us were starting to know, because clearly she had never met *herself*. This is what I wrote:

"Everyone experiences days...seasons that just suck. We all have felt unsatisfied by our work, overwhelmed with the issues of life, frustrated in relationships and lost in our purpose and direction. We all go through personal disappointment, whether by the actions of others or by what we've brought on ourselves. It's easy for us to get in a cycle that repeats over and over, to the point that we stop expecting a change and we give up on trying to change. Trust me, we have all been there. I've been there.

When I was younger in life and in ministry, people would always ask me what was wrong with me - why I was always frowning, why I was so negative, why I didn't speak, etc., etc. Well, it was because I was dealing with immeasurable insecurity, low self-esteem and regret. I had 'friends,' but I always felt so alone. I knew the Word of God, but I was still immature in my faith and struggled with confidence in myself. Then one day I just made a conscious decision to change. I started paying attention to myself. I knew when I was acting or was about to act ugly and I would choose not to before anyone else had to tell me. Even now, if I'm not careful, I can easily slip back into that negative mode since it was my way of guarding myself from people's opinions and from my own emotions. I remind myself all the time, that negative person is not who I am or who I want to be. I make myself respond differently.

The Garden of Gethsemane was a very real place. Throughout His life, Christ felt the same frustrations that we feel. His friends were trifling. He was broke. He was lonely and couldn't please everyone. While we're losing our composure in a choir rehearsal, Christ had a complete meltdown in Gethsemane. Nevertheless, He made the choice to get it together, to accept the hard road ahead and to leave all the past disappointments behind. He had to do what had to be done for the sake of the world. As ministers (which you and I are), as public figures (which we are) and as leaders (which we are) we make the choice to do what has to be done for the sake of the world around us. One of the greatest realizations I've come to with regard to ministry is that sometimes we want to do it out of desire and other times we have to do it out of obligation. I think that's that little fine print God slipped in there when the word says sacrifice our reasonable service. Who wants to sacrifice self-preservation for as a way of life? But it's that sacrifice that separates those who are fulfilling the call on their life from those who have settled for remaining hidden in the shadows. Those shadow dwellers are who I call the comfortably unsatisfied. Still, I've learned that accepting the call on my life and staying committed is also where my heavenly reward and earthly blessings come from. So, yes, we do put on happy faces in public and speak hope to those around us and then cry for ourselves when we get home. Yes, we lead the masses with strength and dignity and then in private we rest on the shoulders of those who care about us. Yes, we speak with confidence and grace as we handle Kingdom business and we find healthy outlets to vent our frustrations at the end of our ministry day. We trust those who lead us to always have our back and our best interests at heart even when their actions don't seem to show it.

Now, you talk about mistakes and guilt? *Girl Please!* No one knows more about it than me. I have willingly put myself in so many situations over the years, knowing that I'd hate myself afterward. It is only by God's grace that I am not locked up in a crazy house. And I'm not being funny. Although we may not serve forgetful people, we do serve a forgiving God. So

I learned to brush myself off and to daily work on getting it together. Truth be told, I put myself on a thirty-one-day consecration in order to begin to address and change the things I hate about myself. No one could make me do it. I had to want to. To this day, I'm learning to have discipline over my emotions, my desires and my actions. And it's working.

Imani, the fellowship choir I started and still direct now, is a safe place. It always has been. For 20 years now, I've taken refuge in this choir. I know God knew that I was getting ready to make a mess of my life time and time again. I believe He ordained the right group of people for each season I was in, to love me through my mess. EVERY traumatic experience in my life, I made it through with my Imani family. They didn't even know about all of it, since many things were too painful or shameful for me to share. But Imani was the one place I never had to hide or pretend. I could be free. I could be happy. I could be strengthened and encouraged. I could be empowered. I could find my purpose again. So, I kept going, I kept getting stronger, I kept getting wiser and I'm still here. See, I discovered that ministry is so much more than music. Ministry is life-giving. Now I'm able to lead with a consistent lifestyle and use my experiences to help other ministers meet themselves.

Now, don't fool yourself. You are absolutely not the same person you were a few years ago. You have done better and you'll continue to grow in every area of your life, *if* you don't give up. You don't learn to walk in wisdom overnight. You don't gain the confidence and respect of the community because of one successful event. You don't develop healthy relationships by remaining guarded. All of it takes work. You've started that work and now you just have to commit to seeing the process through. Trust me, if you do you will love the person you become. And that's true happiness.

I think I've run out of words here, but I hope something in this long letter made sense and encourages you to keep pressing. Always know that if I didn't care about you and if your future didn't matter to me, I wouldn't correct you. It's when you stop receiving correction from God and from those who love you that you should begin to worry.

Everyone deserves to experience their greatest potential in life. That includes you. And I'm committed to helping you on that journey, if you let me.

Love you. And I expect to see the better you real soon, on the other side of this."

Chapter 7 - I Declare War

In the 46 years they've been married, my parents raised 16 biological and adopted children. We were kind of like the Brady Bunch except without the blended family dynamic - oh and we didn't have a maid. We all grew up with the same mom, same dad, a dog, a cat and whole bunch of crazy kids. When I was about 7 years old my mom came up with a special way of letting me know when an addition to our family was about to take place. As I would leave for school in the morning she would say, "When you get home there's something on television I want you to watch." It was an ABC Afterschool Special called *My Mom's Having a Baby* which was about a 10-year-old boy named Petey. After learning his mom was pregnant with his soon to be baby brother he began to seek answers to where babies came from. He also started to realize that he was about to be the oldest of a sibling group of two. I could relate to Petey and the significant impact the birth of his baby brother had on his life. It was like my world was being invaded by aliens every three or four years after that. The only warning I had that these trespassers were on their way, was the oddly coincidental re-runs of *My Mom's Having a Baby* that my mom kept making me watch every few years. The role of being the oldest brother came with a lot of responsibility but not without certain [unofficial] perks. When I was left to babysit my siblings I did absolutely nothing and made them do everything. Maybe I was incorrect earlier. We did have maids, my siblings! If there was laundry that needed to be done, I supervised while they washed, dried, folded and put the laundry away. I decided who deserved to go to bed early and deserved to stay up late. If I was thirsty I would use our intercom system, which was really the vent in the floor that I yelled through to call for one of my siblings to bring me a cool beverage as I relaxed in the TV room. I ran the house the way I thought it should be run if I were in charge. The only problem with that was that I had no real authority and I usually got in trouble once my parents came home. But the living was good while it lasted.

I don't know why, but it seemed as though my siblings still held a grudge even after our parents would return home and my reign of power was over. We would be upstairs in one of our rooms arguing or fighting because they were threatening to expose my wrong doing to our parents. Well I couldn't let that happen. So I would just offer them a little ten cent bribe or some penny candy and that would usually resolve the situation. They were so gullible. But as they got older and started refusing my bribes, the arguments would get so heated that the sound of sibling rivalry would travel throughout the house. Before we knew it, we would hear mom's footsteps running up the stairs followed by her loud alto voice shouting, "Peace, peace, but there is no peace. The war has just begun!" Saying random things like this was one of our mom's many peculiarities. To us she was the smartest woman in the entire universe but we had no idea what she was talking about sometimes. Whether we understood her rants or not, when the door swung open our mother would be standing there declaring war on us if we didn't shut up all that arguing.

That phrase she would often shout was taken from a speech made by Patrick Henry in 1775. When Gwendolyn Townsend said it in the 1980's, it took on a whole new meaning for us. When chaos broke out in our home, it was my mother who set things in order. No matter how big and bad we thought we were, she reminded us that all power was in her hands -literally. If we still would not comply, she would declare nuclear war by saying, "That's all right. Just wait until your father gets home!" Now why would we want to wait for that? Didn't she know self-preservation was the first rule of nature? We wanted to live!

It was order and discipline like that that kept my siblings and I sheltered and protected from a lot of bad choices. Our parents taught us that we could always call on them when we were faced with problems too big for us to handle alone. That same peculiar mother who seemed irrational to us when it came to our own discipline, and that same father whose swing of the belt seemed to have the strength of a gladiator - they were exactly who we called on throughout our lives when we needed giant slayers. Growing up, they were always our champions.

In John the sixteenth chapter, Jesus reminded His disciples who He really was and the joy and peace that belonged to them because they loved Him. Verses

29-33 say, "Then Jesus' disciples said, "Now you are speaking clearly and without figures of speech. Now we can see that you know all things and that you do not even need to have anyone ask you questions. This makes us believe that you came from God." "Do you now believe?" Jesus replied. "A time is coming and in fact has come when you will be scattered, each to your own home. You will leave me all alone. Yet I am not alone, for my Father is with me. "I have told you these things, so that in me you may have peace. In this world you will have trouble. But take heart! I have overcome the world." (NIV)

Christ reminds us that life is not always going to be easy but we should never fear because we will always have the Greater within us. The Greater can fight every battle and win! When we face anything we think we can't handle, our prayers summon the power of God to work on our behalf. Every weapon of the enemy has been rendered ineffective by the death, burial, and resurrection of Christ. "I have given you authority... to overcome all the power of the enemy." (Luke 10:19, NIV). Christ is with us so that in this life, no matter what the test, we can walk in peace.

As Christians, we are to demonstrate that same strength, command of situations and compassion when those around us experience seasons of chaos, which will indeed come. When the disciples were on a ship and the winds and the waves began to threaten the journey, it was Jesus who came up from the bottom of the ship and said, "Peace be still." Christ is no amateur at rising up from the depths of our soul and despair and speaking peace to the storms of our lives. Likewise, we are to become peacemakers in the lives of those around us. As Christ-like believers we should specialize in bringing calm to chaos, not creating more. I think the eleventh commandment should have been Thou Shalt not use Social Media to get even. Social Media has become sharp stones in the hands of self-righteous so called Christians who have forgotten their own season in the dirt. The war we are fighting should not be with one another but against the enemy whose sole mission is to divide, conquer and destroy the family of God. If we don't get it together our Heavenly Father is going to get all of us when He gets home. And trust me, like my dad, our Heavenly Father is no amateur at discipline either. When God starts swingin' my advice is to duck and run.

Chapter 8 - The Little Black Book

The Facebook message started with, "Sam Townsend are you online?"

I replied, "Yup, on my phone, wassup?"

She said, "Nothing, just bored. Decided to do a little harassing."

Jokingly, I answered, "Lol...oh lord. Why not go pass out tracts? Jesus is coming soon."

"I ain't got none," she responded. "I passed them all out in the 1990s. Once they're gone...oh well. But you should print some so our choir can go hit the streets one Saturday. You lead."

"Hmmm...." I replied. "I'll get right on that. Lol."

In what year did witnessing go out of style and anticipating Christ's return become a joke? Last time I checked, the Lord's command to go out into the highways and hedges and compel men and women to come to Him never had an expiration date. There was a time not very long ago, maybe in the 90s, when it seemed that "He's coming back" was all we talked about. We sported bumper stickers on our cars with the fish symbol, or we wore sweatshirts that said "I heart Jesus." We proudly placed our biggest Bible on our work desk, daring anyone to challenge us to remove it. In our cars, we weren't ashamed to blast Gospel music while waiting at red lights with our windows rolled down.

FUNNY FAITH

Nowadays, it seems like we spend more energy preparing ourselves for a long and prosperous life here on earth, rather than trying to prepare the world for eternity. We've all seen the man on the street with the sign saying, "The End is Coming" or "The Lord will return in... [well, you name the year]." Although the Lord has been gracious in His delay to return, I guarantee you, He is still coming back. When I was a kid I didn't like the idea of not knowing when Jesus would return. One scripture my dad drilled in my head was Luke 12:40 NIV, "You also must be ready, because the Son of Man will come at an hour when you do not expect him." Well I just thought that was awfully sneaky of Jesus. But I had a plan, a loop hole if you will. As a child, anytime I did something bad, like stealing gum out of my mom's purse, I would just repeat in my head, "He's coming, He's coming, He's coming." I figured that if I kept thinking about Him coming back, He couldn't. I know it was foolish childhood logic, but some of us grown folks have some foolish ideas too.

I remember in July 1980, after our family left the large, beautiful, thriving church where my parents had accepted Christ, Tolliver Temple COGIC; my dad started our church, Greater Glory COGIC. I was ten years old and I was not happy about this transition at all. I remember when my dad first told me that the name of our church would be Greater Glory. I thought to myself, "well that's just the dumbest church name I've ever heard. It's supposed to be 'something church', or 'something temple', like where we came from. But 'Greater – Glory?' Who does that!" As new disgruntled P.K.'s (Pastor's Kids), my younger brother Gregg and I became Junior Deacons. Really, with only six adult members and their children when we started, my brother and I were junior everything. Gregg was 3 ½ years younger than I was and every Sunday we fulfilled our Junior Deacon roles by setting up the red metal chairs in the basement of the rented house that served as our sanctuary. In Seattle, even in the summer it was cold and rainy so the basement of the house church was perpetually damp and smelled of mildew. But my dad was proud of the ministry he had started and the tiny congregation of six faithfully worshipped every Sunday and once a week for bible study. I remember one night as we arrived for bible study, we walked down the slippery concrete steps that lead to the basement from outside and we found that the basement was completely flooded by the rain. I thought to myself, "Good! We're going home!" *Nope* - My dad, my mom and the four others; Sis. Debbie, Brother and Sister Carty, and Sis. Sharon all began to grab what they could and we moved upstairs to the living room of the rented house. The living room which my dad had intended to turn into a family counseling center became our new sanctuary. This turned out to be a blessing because there was a fireplace upstairs, as well as more light than in the basement. It was hard to go from the big cathedral like church we had grown up in, to a dark basement of a leaky house. So, although the living room wasn't a cathedral, it beat the basement.

After Gregg and I set up the red metal chairs we would go outside and find whatever dry wood was around for the fireplace so we could help keep the saints warm. We didn't have a Hammond B-3 organ. We didn't have a grand chandelier or stage lights. We didn't have stained glass windows. We didn't have the space or the budget to host revivals and musicals. We didn't have the structure or membership to have a list of ministry programs. What we did have was a purpose driven pastor, my dad. Since the rented house was situated in a quiet residential neighborhood on the hill it didn't really represent the look of traditional church and it didn't attract much attention. So my dad decided we would literally take the church into the streets.

My dad would gather everyone at the house on Saturday mornings, map out our territory, designate teams and we would go door to door armed with our Bibles and a handful of tracts. Just thinking about it now makes me smile. I started falling in love with the whole idea of starting a church and couldn't wait to canvass the neighborhood with my dad, my pastor. It's funny how God can turn a burden into passion and turn passion into ministry.

We went door to door passing out tracts, leaving them in mailboxes, stuffing them between fences, sliding them in door jambs and leaving them on car windshields. That was only when someone didn't answer their front door. Oh yes, we literally went knocking door to door. We were bold back then. Nothing stopped us, not even a "Beware of Dog" sign. We just made sure we made noise before entering the gate and if we didn't hear barking, we walked right up to the door and knocked.

My dad was a pro when it came to witnessing. He had a way of approaching complete strangers and talking to them about Christ in such an inviting and convincing manner. People would stand in their doorways and listen to everything he had to say. When he felt he had said enough, he'd say a simple prayer with them and leave them with a tract that he had written our house-church address on. We would leave and he would say, "Son, the rest is up to God." Well, at least it was up to God until the next Saturday, because there were a few houses I remember my dad went to more than once.

My dad didn't restrict himself to our house-church neighborhood either. He canvassed areas all over the city of Seattle. He and some preacher friends of his, Minster Henry Jenkins and Minister Charles Ruffin, who were still members of Tolliver Temple, would go to some of the roughest areas of downtown Seattle. Folks would be getting off work, rushing to their cars or to catch a bus and would seem to pay them no mind. Some would be smoking, walking the streets with a bottle of alcohol in their hand on their way to their favorite Friday night bar. No matter how busy and distracted everyone else seemed, my dad would just post himself on the corner and start singing, "Good News! Good News! I've got Good News! Good News!" That was the chant he would sing loud and boldly with a smile on his face, a Bible in one hand, tracts in the other hand and my brother Gregg and I by his side.

We watched our parents share the Word and the love of God with people and they made it seem so exciting, that as kids we wanted in. So, instead of only keeping our parents company, my brother and I started taking our own Bibles and handfuls of tracts. It started as more of a competition than a ministry for us. We would see who could hit the most houses in the short hour or two we had on Saturdays, or which one of us would be first to get a wino downtown to take a tract from us on a Friday night. We equated witnessing and passing out tracts to the number of jewels in our heavenly crowns. I guess we won't really know who won until we get to heaven but I'll probably need armored security for my crown. I'm just saying. I put in work! Even so, the more my brother and I went out witnessing with our parents or the church family, the more we developed a love for sharing God's Word with people. We started to experience the same joy our parents felt. It was the joy of knowing that we were doing the will of God in sharing His message of love to people who may have never heard it. It wasn't only His message of love but also His promise to return for His people.

I would ask, "Dad, how do we know when Jesus is coming back?" He would say, "We don't know when. No one does. But He won't come back until every single person on earth has had an opportunity to hear and receive the message of salvation." He said when the last person on earth had his or her opportunity to accept Him as their savior, Christ would return. That made enough sense to us as children and we wanted to do our part to make sure no one was left behind including us. On New Year's Eve every year our dad would show the 1972 Christian end times film *A Thief in the Night* to the church. In this movie it depicted what it would be like when the rapture happens. There was a scene with a little girl crossing the street carrying a carton of eggs. Suddenly the rapture happened and all you saw in the next scene were eggs in the street! No girl. Scared us to death. Back then, we really did live into the old song by Andrae Crouch & the Disciples, "It Won't Be Long." We expected Christ to return at any moment.

In the early 1970's, when my dad got saved, he left the Seattle Police force and began to serve as a Sr. Community Service Officer, handling a lot of the domestic disturbance cases in the city that social workers handle now. He would often take me to ride with him on his calls. Sometimes, we would go out in the middle of the day to visit with a bedridden senior citizen, or we would go at midnight to transport a drug addict to a rehabilitation center. While waiting in the car for my dad one day, I found a little black book under his seat. Yes, I was the son of a preacher, but I was still a nosey little kid. The hard, black cover of the book was worn, the pages were brown on the edges and when I opened the book, every single page, front and back was filled with first and last names random people. Random, so I thought. There were hundreds of names, none of which I recognized. When my dad got back in the car, I asked him what the book was. He told me, "Those are the names of every person I've witnessed to. I write them in the book, I pray for them and when it's possible, I go to check on them." Then he showed me several black books, each one with worn pages lined from top to bottom, front to back with names of people he had witnessed to. They were souls he intended to win for Christ.

I want to go back to those days, living and believing that on any day, Christ could break through the clouds. I want to find the courage to share the love of Christ when it's not convenient, outside of the pulpit of my church and the safety of other believers. I want to find the passion again to boldly share the Good News with strangers whom I may never see again and let them know that there's an answer for whatever they may be facing in life. I want to feel the anxious joy of knocking on doors, standing on corners, visiting the widow and comforting the addict with compassion. I want to serve God and mankind like my father taught me when I was ten years old. Not for an extra jewel in my crown, but for a soul for the Kingdom.

Today, I went to the gas station and as I pulled in I heard the Spirit say, "Go to the other side." Without questioning why, I went. I passed the first few open pumps and pulled up to where I felt the Spirit told me to stop. Still unsure why, I got out of my car and went around to start pumping my gas and the Spirit led me to look up. I noticed a cane leaning against a gas pump across from me. A few feet away was an old beat up green truck getting ready to pull off. Hurrying, I left my car and as I approached the open driver's side window of the truck, I said, "Excuse me, sir, did you just leave this pump?"

The elderly man in the truck answered, "Yes, I did."

"I think you left your cane," I told him. I ran back to the pump for the cane and I handed it to the man through the window. As he turned his head to say thank you I noticed an oxygen tank and the tube in his nose. Deciding to operate in this revived 1970's evangelistic boldness, I shared with the man that "it must have been the Lord Who called me to this side of the gas station, just to help him."

The man replied, "Yes, the Lord works in devious ways." I think he meant "mysterious." As he drove off, I began to pray for him and asked the Lord to cover him, to touch his health and to give him long life. I thanked the Lord for directing me and giving me an opportunity to share what I could with the man before he rushed off and I asked the Lord to continue sending Christians in the man's path to minister in some way to him until he'd have an opportunity to hear the full message of God's love. I never knew the man's name and I may never see him again, but if I had a little black book I would write, "Man in the green truck."

When was the last time you heard and obeyed the voice of the Lord telling you to go to the other side, to leave the familiarity of your neighborhood, or the comfort of your house church? The next line of your little black book is waiting, somewhere out there.

Chapter 9 - You Look A Mess

As a kid playing with my neighborhood friends, I would often find myself trying to outdo everyone else. I wanted to be able to run faster, climb higher, hide longer - you name it, I wanted to do it better. Whether it was who had the fastest ten speed bike, who got the best grade on a math quiz, or who got the most money on Christmas, I was dedicated to being the kid with the best story. Unfortunately, I rarely did have the best story but that didn't stop me from aiming high. Eventually, my friends grew weary of tolerating my narcissistic behavior and they would shut me down with seven magic words: "We'll believe it when we see it." Still, I tried to stay on top and save face. For example, once when I wasn't able to prove that I had twenty-five dollars in my pocket, I said, "No, I said twenty-five doll-hairs!" It wasn't the cleverest lie but I was only a kid. I learned to lie better as I got older. I also began to realize more and more that people were not going to just believe what I said, they wanted proof. So the lying stopped and I learned to accept and speak my truth.

There's a popular phrase that many believers have adopted as their mantra, "I'm glad I don't look like what I've been through." Particularly in the Pentecostal church, when we think of the goodness of Jesus and all he has done for us, all we need is a Hammond B-3 organ and one of those young guys on the drums with some stamina and we'll dance and shout ourselves into a Holy Ghost frenzy. For those who are rhythmically challenged, a couple of leaps in place or a few laps around the church will do. We've written songs about the phrase and have used it in our testimonies. I don't know how many times during one of those fiery sermons, I've been told to turn to my neighbor and say it... (And, by the way, I absolutely hate being told to talk to my neighbor twenty times during a service. I just want some alone time in church.)

You know, the more I'd hear the phrase, "I'm glad I don't look like what I've been through," the more it just didn't work for me. The apostle Paul did said we're supposed to forget those things that are behind us, reach for the things that are before us and press toward the mark (Philippians 3:12-14.) But I think some of us Christians run so fast that the world is only able to see us clearly *after* we have arrived at the finish line, celebrating our victory. Everything else before that is a blur. We tend to hide and shout over all the times we ran in the wrong direction, even though the correct route had been plainly laid out for us. We minimize the number of times we fell down and we don't even mention the number of lives we took down with us. Physically I'm a slender guy, but spiritually I was once so morbidly obese with the guilt and shame of my past that it took me years to get in the right condition to even start running the race. Laying aside every weight and sin is sometimes easier said than done. Although I didn't like the person I had become, I was too ashamed to admit it and I began to use the duties of ministry to dull emotional pain. My testimony was that I was walking in complete victory. I led praise and worship, directed the choir and played the organ like I was living the best life. I broke out of the pews and danced with the rest of the church. I preached and worked the altar telling the struggling people that I believed God could do anything. But I didn't really believe that for myself. Honestly, I started to think things like, "God, after all I've done for you in ministry, is this is how you're going treat me?" I'm sure God sat on the edge of his throne a few times saying, "Gabriel, hold me back! This boy must have lost his mind!"

One night, I found myself in a deep state of depression. In addition to having some internal conflicts and emotional wounds that I still needed healing from, I was hospitalized and bedridden off and on for several weeks. I was recuperating from major surgery. I had been diagnosed with Ulcerative Colitis which had spread so aggressively that my colon and entire large intestine had to be removed in order to eradicate the high risk of Colon Cancer. On this particular night I looked at my body in the mirror and I didn't recognize who I was. My face was sunk in and my body was frail from the amount of weight and blood loss before and after the surgery. I could see all the wounds left from the scalpels, surgical stitches and staples. The most prominent was the scar that was almost a foot long across my abdomen where the doctors had performed the total colectomy. Then there were the wounds in my left side where tubes had been inserted to drain the fluid after surgery.

There were the wounds in my chest and my left arm where tubes had been inserted to administer larger doses of medication than was possible intravenously. I looked at my disfigured body and thought about how tired I was of walking by faith. I began to cry out loud, asking God, "Why me? Why didn't you miraculously heal me like you do everyone else? Why are you making me go through all this pain? After all the preaching and ministering that I've done, why do I still have to struggle with all these issues that I never asked for, emotionally, spiritually and physically? Why does it feel like your answer to me is always 'no'?"

If I had never heard the Lord speak before, I heard him that night. He said, "Because I knew I could trust you with the scars." It wasn't until then that I realized there was a divine purpose in me looking exactly like what I had been through. God knew that even as broken as I was in heart, body and spirit, I was a fighter and I was committed to serving him and to serving others with my life. He knew He could count on me to use every experience, every struggle, every scar and every pain as motivation to move and speak in faith. Perhaps I had been chosen to suffer as the saints of old who suffered while proclaiming the faithfulness and promises of God, yet never received the promise themselves. Hebrews 11 says that the world was not even worthy of them but they were commended for their faith, never receiving the promise on earth, because God had something better for them in eternity. Perhaps, I am one of them and started taking courage in that possibility.

Not very long after that night, I attended a musical that my Imani Fellowship Choir ministry had planned before my ordeal. I just had to get out of that house even if it was against the doctor's orders. I was so weak and in so much pain at the musical that it took two people on each side to help me walk slowly down the aisle. It was the first time I had been seen by the public for about two months and someone asked me, "Why are you here? You look a mess!" Now if I wasn't a Christian I would have asked her why she was there since her raggedy weave had been recalled. But I digress. I didn't want to tarnish my witness. God knows my heart.

Midway through the musical, it was time for Imani to sing. Everyone tried to talk me out of directing but I had something to prove. I was pale, anemic, bent over, holding my stomach where the wounds hurt the most, barely able to walk and unable to stand very long. I sat in a chair someone had brought me and I directed and led the familiar song by Jonathan Nelson, "My Name is Victory." I sang it until I couldn't sing it no more. That night I testified that I still trusted God. That night I agreed with God and said he could trust me with the scars.

My dad preached a message one Sunday that said it all, "You may not get out of it, you may not get over it, but you will get through it." I've learned that no matter what comes my way, if God allows it to happen, He has plans to use it for His glory. You would be amazed how the most jacked up part of your life can turn into the greatest testimony if you put it in God's hands. You don't need to dress up your past and your pain so much that even you forget where you came from. There is someone out there who's going through exactly what you came through or are yet dealing with. There is a woman still haunted by how she was violated. There is a young man struggling with his sexual identity. There's a child angry because the foster system has failed him. There's a preacher who has publicly fallen from grace. There is a pastor whose marriage is on the rocks. There's a believer who has lost faith. There's a sinner who's exactly what you were. Church folks can at times be too insensitive and undiscerning to know when to preach and when to just love. That's why God needs a witness like you. That's why He needs someone with the scars to say, "Look at me. If I can make it, so can you. This is how, and we can do it together."

John 20:25 (NIV) says, "So the other disciples told him, "We have seen the Lord!" But he (Thomas) said to them, "Unless I see the nail marks in his hands and put my finger where the nails were, and put my hand into his side, I will not believe."

I've learned that there are so many people just like Thomas. When he was told by the other disciples that Christ had risen from the dead, he wasn't trying to hear it. He had the same response as my childhood friends, "I'll believe it when I see it." It took Jesus Himself to expose the wound in his side and to extend his nail-scarred hands to Thomas before he would believe.

As born-again believers, we need to be willing to do the same. Our lives need to be transparent enough that the world can see the power of Christ in us. Even when God's answer for us seems to be "no," His promises are always "yes." He promised that His grace would be sufficient to carry us through. So, I'm glad that in some ways, I look *exactly* like what I've been through. I've earned these scars and the anointing they carry. The question is, can God trust you with your scars?

Chapter 10 - Church Boy

I've been in church all my life. At Tolliver Temple COGIC I sang in the youth choir and Minister Ronelle McGraw, our Minister of Music, and his wife Sister Mary Jean McGraw, our organist, gave me my first choir solo, "Up Above My Head I Hear Music in the Air." Minister McGraw was also the first person to influence me as a Choir Director. I was always a Shepherd or a Wiseman in the Christmas plays and I always knew my speech for the Easter program. Yes, I was a church boy. My parents took my siblings and me to Sunday School at 9:45am every Sunday and I couldn't wait until I got in the older kids' class because they had their classes in the balcony – which was so cool.

The 11:30am service at Tolliver Temple was always jumpin', but it was so long. Sometimes, I would keep myself awake by turning to the side and pretending the armrest of my seat was an organ and I would mimic Sis. McGraw. When Pastor James got long winded with his preaching, because the church used to be a Jewish synagogue, I would sit and count the Stars of David that lined the walls of the balcony. If my eyes were still getting heavy, I would stare at the enormous crystal-beaded chandelier that hung over the three hundred seat sanctuary, imagining how I would leap into action like Superman if the chandelier started to fall on someone below while they were shouting. I always had a great imagination. After service, my siblings and I would go upstairs into the dining hall and eat the lunch that our mom had packed for us in Tupperware containers. It seemed like that was our ritual every Sunday. Then we would be hurried right back into church for a 3:00pm service. Whose idea was it to create 3:00pm services, anyway? Sunday is the Sabbath. Give Jesus a break. Ugh.

If that wasn't enough, we had to attend Y.P.W.W. (Young People Willing Workers) at 6:00pm and Sunday night service at 7:30pm. Yes, I was a certified church boy. Even as a teenager after my dad started pastoring, I never played sports in high school because I had to go to choir rehearsal. That's why to this day I can't play any sports that require me to shoot, dribble, kick, catch, throw, tackle, jump, hit or run. My mom did enroll my brother Gregg and I into tumbling classes for several years when I was around seven years old. I never guessed that learning to do those flips and random arm movements would come in handy years later as choir director. I never went to a movie theater until I was an adult and married because I had to attend weeknight Bible studies. Back then, the saints also taught us that it was a sin to go to the "picture show" because that's where folks "make-out." Ironically, I do have a vague memory of a drive-in movie my parents took my brother Gregg and I to see titled *The Nude Bomb*. I'm not sure how they missed the plot from the title, but it was sure was funny when we got there. Google it. I never attended a dance at school until my prom and even that night my parents made the limo driver bring my prom date Arika, who would later become my wife and the mother of our son Talorien, to Friday night service first. Who does that? I don't even think Arika and I ever kissed until the night I proposed and even then I was waiting for my mom to come leaping off the porch shouting, "loose here Satan". Some people may think my parents were too extreme. Well, maybe they were a little. But remember, they had gotten saved in the 70's when they were both in their early twenties. My mom being raised Catholic and my dad, well he was just from the streets. When they came to Christ, neither of them had any experience in holiness. So, whatever the saints at Tolliver Temple taught them was right, that's what they did and that's what they taught their children. A love for God and church was mandatory in our house. Raising us in church was the best way, the only way they knew to protect us from as much of the evils of the world as they could. They both knew a thing or two about life outside of Christ and that wasn't the life they wanted for us. Hence, they raised a church boy.

To put all this into perspective, I think I should tell you the story of how my parents came to Christ. My dad, who was stationed at Ft. Lewis Army base, met my mom and her best friend Sharon one night while they were on base. My mom and Sharon noticed my dad coming out of the mess hall and asked him for something to eat. Although my dad was a chef, he had already shut the kitchen down and all he had to offer them was bananas and milk. They accepted. To show how God works, the street in Ft. Lewis where my parents met that night was Faith Avenue. My mom's best friend Sharon would later become one of the original six charter members of our church and over 45 years later she is currently one of the church mothers. Just two weeks after the night of bananas and milk on Faith Avenue, my dad proposed to my mom but she declined and "disappeared." I already told you all, she was a peculiar woman. With great persistence, my dad found her, won her heart and they would be married a year and a half later. Now because my mom was a Catholic girl, in order for their union to be approved both my parents had to vow to also raise their children Catholic. My dad, who had absolutely no intention of doing so, lied and said that he would. He was not going to lose the girl of his dreams a second time and I don't think the charm of bananas and milk would have worked on the priest. Well, the priest bought it. He married them and when I was born I was baptized Catholic. So technically from birth, I was destined to be a church boy. That doesn't mean I've been saved since conception. Neither were you! No matter the religious ritual or even how far north our moral compass points, until we accept Christ as our Savior, we are all just sinners - plain and simple. I know no one wants to be called a "sinner", but I grew up in a time when it was just the honest truth. Although it was never used in malice, it was the most direct way the church knew to point out the true nature of a person's soul. The wonderful thing about God is that He loves us as we are and not based on who he wants us to be. His love is so strong that once we accept it, it changes us into who we should be.

My mom and dad came to the Lord in very peculiar ways. After my dad was discharged from the army, he became a Seattle Police officer. He used to get his hair cut (and his afro wig trimmed) every week at Kelly's Barbershop. Mr. Kelly, who was also a preacher at Tolliver Temple, would witness to my dad every week, trying to get him to go to church. On one particular day in February, Mr. Kelly asked my dad, "If it's the Lord's will, will you come to church?" Never anticipating that he'd have to follow through, my dad sarcastically answered, "Sure." As my dad was walking out the door, Mr. Kelly replied, "It is the Lord's will." I'm sure Mr. Kelly and the Lord had a good laugh right then.

When Sunday came around, my dad found himself rolling down the street in his Buick Rivera (the Rive Dawg, as he called it), dressed in an all red bellbottomed suit, platform shoes and freshly styled afro wig tapered into his own hair. He had his police gun, his badge and some drugs in the trunk of the car and he was headed to Mr. Kelly's church. He gave a whole new meaning to "coming as you are." My dad was a cold piece of work. When he pulled up to the big brick church he realized he recognized the area. The church was located on Yesler Avenue in the Central District of Seattle, one of the neighborhoods that he patrolled as a policeman. Although he was use to responding to sounds of violence and distress from homes on the block, what he heard coming from the church through its stained glass windows was something very different. He could hear music, the voices of people singing, shouting and rejoicing. Since he hadn't been raised in church, he instinctively decided that when he got inside he was going to just sit and watch. My dad strolled through the double doors of the sanctuary, cool, calm and collected. He had one of those 1970 struts that was a combination of a subtle hop with one leg while you kind-of dragged the other leg and then waited for it to catch up. One of the elders of the church (who later became my father's closest friend, Elder John Heflin) noticed my dad walking in. He said to another preacher, "That dude right there ain't gonna get nothing from the Lord. He's too cool."

Well, Elder Heflin was partially correct. My dad was cool. He doesn't remember what the sermon was about or what the choir sang that day, but he does remember that he was intrigued that there were so many young people his age in church. They all seemed happy and that music was really good! When it came time for the altar call, an old Church Mother named Sarah Jenkins approached him. Her son, Minister Henry Jenkins would later become my dad's best friend and her daughter, Sister McGraw the church organist, would later become one of my mentors. Mother Jenkins was a short bowlegged black woman with dark skin. She was dressed in all white, her gray hair was covered in a tightly fitted white turban, white stockings knotted up at her knees and white shoes on her feet. She wasn't intimidated by his posture, his red suit, his platform shoes or his afro. Even though she was a woman of short stature, she looked up at him square in his eyes and said with a raspy high pitched voice that would crescendo at the end of the question, "Young man, do you want to be saved?"

Despite having not been raised in church, my dad's Pentecostal mother and Baptist father from Grand Rapids, Michigan, by way of Tupelo, Mississippi, had still taught him to always respect his elders. So, despite how insincere he was, he answered, "Yes, ma'am." With perfect godly timing just like Mr. Kelly, as she turned and walked away the next words that came from Mother Jenkins mouth changed my dad's life forever. She said, "Then tell God about it."

The older saints were tarrying at the altar with the other young people. How tarrying worked was, depending on what the saints discerned you needed, that's what they would get in your ear and yell. Seemingly right into your spirit they would shout "Give it up! Turn it loose! Hold on! Let it go! Higher Lord! Loose the mind! Say Yes Lord!" Whatever they said, you said. This wasn't just some type of hypnotic chanting. It was, and still is how millions of saints, at least those of the Church of God in Christ for over 100 years now learned to follow and yield to the Holy Spirit. The act of tarrying at the altar taught us to block out the distracting voice of the devil, and focus only on the breakthrough in Christ that we were desperately seeking.

My dad found his way to the altar, to tell God about it as Mother Jenkins had instructed. Since he only followed through out of respect, he just started repeating whatever he heard everyone else saying.

"Save me Jesus, save me Jesus, save me - Jesus…" The tarrying service seemed to take on a life of its own. "Save me Jesus, save me Jesus, save me - Jesus…" A melody from the guitar, piano, organ and an upbeat cadence from the drum began to swell, filling the room. "Save me Jesus, save me Jesus, save me - Jesus…" Now it seemed like everyone in the sanctuary was singing it in concert, "Save me Jesus, save me Jesus, save me - Jesus…"

Within a few minutes my dad went from merely mimicking everyone around him to dropping to the floor and rolling under the organ under the power of the Holy Ghost, weeping, "Save me Jesus! Save me - Jesus!" The rest is history. That Monday, my dad went to work, laid his gun and badge down on the sergeant's desk and quit the police force. A few months later, he started preaching the Gospel.

Now, my mom's story is a little different. Before my dad got saved he had a habit of disappearing and partying all weekend, leaving my mother and little baby me at home alone. He usually came back home on Sundays. Well, my mom had had enough one weekend, which happened to be the Sunday he was at the altar giving his life to Christ. When my dad came home from church all excited, telling her that he got saved, my mom, with her bags already packed and at the door, replied, "…Great." While carrying me on her hip, she started putting her bags in the car. Still trying to convince my mom that he had changed, my dad began taking the bags back out of the car. Every time he took a bag out, my mom put another bag in. He could have said he was saved until he was blue in the face. My Catholic mom didn't know anything about salvation and frankly she was fed up with my dad's disappearing act.

Eventually, my mom's decision to leave prevailed. With little baby me and her bags in the car, she drove to my grandparents' house. A few hours later, my dad showed up. Following a long conversation with my mom, my grandmother and my grandfather who just so happened to be a Seattle Police captain, my dad somehow convinced everyone that something in his heart had changed. So, my mom returned home with him. She said we lived out of suitcases for the next two months, just in case this "salvation" thing didn't pan out and my dad went back to his old ways.

My mom started attending church services with my dad the very next week. Although she didn't understand it, she did her best to tolerate the very loud Pentecostal experience as well as accepting the new disciplines of holiness the church was teaching. She attended service every Sunday and mid-week Bible studies and she even joined the choir. She was still very much Catholic, with rosary beads and all. Then in December of that same year, while sitting in the choir stand, the choir director stood to introduce the choir's next selection. Much like my father, my mom doesn't recall the exact words he used but how ever he expressed the meaning of the song was enough to change the course of my mom's life. Right there, sitting in the choir stand, listening to what the choir director was saying about God's love for us, she sat pondering it in her heart. My Catholic mother gave her life to the Lord in the quietness of that moment. No tarrying at the altar. No Hammond B-3 organ. No euphoric burst of emotion - just an inward decision influenced by the sincere, anointed words of a choir director.

It wasn't based on how a person was dressed, it wasn't about how guilty the saints could make anyone feel about how they were living, and it wasn't for any personal gain or agenda. Mr. Kelly, Mother Jenkins, and Minister McGraw all had the same thing in common: Jeremiah 31:3 (NIV), "I have loved you with an everlasting love; I have drawn you with unfailing kindness." They used genuine compassion and godly wisdom in their direct and indirect communication and it changed lives.

Growing up in church, I've seen so much abuse in the name of religion. I've experienced it personally. I've been called out over the pulpit and not by my name. I've watched innocent, naive visitors be turned off by the rudeness of the saints on Sunday mornings. I've read inappropriate judgments of high profile believers spread all over the Internet. And I think it's sad and a disgrace to the Body of Christ. Where is the love? Where is the patience? Where are the spiritual mothers and fathers like Mother Jenkins and the Mr. Kelly? There are generations of church boys and church girls waiting to be born. Thank God I came through when I did.

My birth name was Larry Craig Townsend. My dad's name is Sam Larry Townsend. In 1989 at the age of 19, because of the amazing example of unconditional love that my father had shown me all my life and because I wanted to be just like him, I changed my name legally to Sam Larry Townsend, Jr. as his Father's Day gift. My dad, with great pride, began to add "Sr." to his name. The love of our Heavenly Father has that same effect. When you begin to realize how He has divinely orchestrated your life to help you become the man or women He has destined you to be, you'll gladly change your identity. You'll no longer desire to live the life a as a "sinner", but rather embrace your new life as a saint of God. You'll go from being a church goer to a church lover. You'll proudly own your new identity as a church boy (or girl), and you'll have your own story to tell... minus the tumbling classes. That's all mine.

Chapter 11 –
My Son is Driving Me Nuts

I know that Jesus was the Son of God and I know that from an early age He was quite aware of His purpose in life. For the most part, according to scripture, He seemed to be pretty well-mannered, obedient to his parents and respectful to men and women. I mean, there was that one awkward moment when He was about twelve years old and Mary and Joseph were searching everywhere for Him and eventually found Him teaching in the temple. I can imagine Mary letting Him have it and Jesus replying, "Don't you know I gotta be about my Father's business?" Yeah... that was awkward. I don't know what happened to Jesus when He got home, but I know we didn't hear from Him again until 18 years later.

I wonder, while the Bible is silent during the adolescent years of Jesus, if Joseph ever screamed, "My son is driving me nuts!" - like I have with my son.

My high school sweetheart Arika and I got married right after we both turned twenty. My son Talorien was born two years later. Arika was much more ready to be a mom and a wife than I was to be a dad and a husband. Even though our marriage only lasted about seven years, we've spent twenty-four amazing years raising our son together. For those who believe the contrary, there *is* life after divorce. Although God hates the separation of a holy union, He can still take the broken pieces and make two vessels of honor, filling them both with His love to perform one single purpose. Our purpose, even being divorced, was to raise our son in the knowledge and love of the Lord. We've done a good job. I mean, we've never had to pick our son up from jail. He hasn't made us grandparents. He's graduated from high school, gainfully employed and aspires to become a music producer. Oh, but those pubescent and adolescent years were no joke. Much like Mary and Joseph, Arika and I had grown up in the same community. We were both popular, well-rounded, responsible, talented and goal-oriented young adults. We were both raised in church, we served as the leaders of the youth ministries and we lived wholesome Christian lives at home. But this guy, Talorien - he was a piece of work.

My son's toddler years were so innocent and gentle. I can remember taking him on picnics, going to the aquarium with him, watching him at T-ball and basketball games. We had this thing called "Making Memories." We'd do something random and out of the ordinary like leave the house late in the evening and follow a spotlight that we saw shining in the sky. Or maybe on our way home from daycare on a rainy day we'd follow a rainbow to see where it ended. One time, my son's fourth grade teacher promised him he could play the drums, which was his passion, in the school concert. For some reason on the day of the event, my son was reassigned to play the triangle. What? He's a Townsend. We ain't playin' no triangle. When my son called me crying I left work and picked him up. After I gave the front desk a piece of my mind, like I think any father would have, I signed my son out of school for the day.

Probably a little afraid that he was in trouble, my son asked where we were going. I just said, with a smile, "We're going to have our own concert." I took him to the newly built Experience Music Project in downtown Seattle, which is basically a high-tech museum of music. I paid for a thirty-minute session. My son got on the drums while I pretended to play guitar and we made a music video. That's what we called *Making Memories*. I told my son never to let anyone tell him he couldn't do something. "If your heart is in it, go out and prove them wrong."

As the little dorky kid in big glasses and braces got older, Talorien became more independent and aware of what he wanted to do in life. And the more independent he became the more he experimented with my grace. I mean, did Jesus ever steal the family camel and drive it until it exploded? Did He ever steal Joseph's shekels from his tent? Did Joseph have to force Jesus to go to carpentry school, or did Jesus naturally develop a love for hammers and nails? Did Jesus sag in His tunic? Well, my son did the 21st Century version of all that. My dad taught me that when the Word of God is silent, you be silent. But I'm sorry, I really need to know what Joseph's secret was or if Jesus really was a perfect little Jewish boy scout. Did he ever miss curfew and have to sleep outside the tent? Talorien has looked up and seen the open sky on a few occasions. My son has tried me in every way possible under the sun. He has a great heart and tremendous ambition. He is so compassionate and respectful to his mother and me. He loves his family and tries to be a great example to his younger cousins and sibling. But as a father, there's so much more I wanted to see him achieve. There are so many headaches, pitfalls and dead ends that I wanted to protect him from. However, he seemed to want to learn everything his own way, the hard way and in his own time. Now, he is a little like Jesus in that he's committed to living out whatever his purpose is. Not everyone understands or agrees with the paths he chooses, but somehow he keeps his head up and never loses his drive. He still drives me nuts sometimes.

On April 29, 1992, the night he was born, I remember experiencing an overwhelming feeling of anxiety. I asked myself, "What if he doesn't like me?" I know that sounds crazy. While sitting in that waiting room before the doctor brought me into the delivery room, I just wanted to say, "Never mind." I wasn't ready but at that point it was too late. Next thing I knew, I was watching my son being born. The doctor tried to hand him to me right away, and I declined, "Uh, no, clean him up first." When I held him and felt his warm body in my arms that was the moment when all fear left me. My little son was here and he was depending on me to nurture him, to protect him, to teach him how to be a man and to teach him how to live and how to love.

My dad and I didn't really have a close relationship during my pubescent and adolescent years. Actually, I only remember our relationship and communication being good up until I was about twelve... and then later on, after I turned about thirty.

That time frame seems familiar. So it was those in-between years that I found to be the hardest to parent my son. I made a personal vow like a lot of men do, to raise my child better than my father raised me. My parents did raise sixteen amazing children. Both of my parents were working full time and both had thriving ministries. So clearly, a lot of what my dad did was right. With me having only one son to raise, I figured it couldn't be that hard. I would just improve on everything my dad taught me.

I was so wrong. There was a period of about two or three years when the relationship between my teenage son and I really suffered. I didn't know how to talk to him and he didn't know how or didn't think he could talk to me. So we didn't talk. In the same house, day after day, existing but never communicating, never connecting. The emotional distance took its toll on us both. One evening when he was about nineteen years old and was staying at his mom's house, he sent a text message to me that was about a billion screens long. The messages kept coming and coming. I don't really know what prompted it, but something in his heart had broken suddenly and he began to share everything he was angry about, everything he was confused about, everything he feared, everything he regretted. Never in our relationship had either of us been that vulnerable. The only thing that ran through my mind was, *my son needs me, and he needs me now.* All I texted back to him was, "Meet me outside in 20 minutes." I jumped in my car and drove to his mom's house. He came outside and as soon as he got in the car and closed the door he burst into uncontrollable tears and fell into my arms. We sat there in the car embracing one another, crying, needing one another. It was the night he was born all over again. My son needed me and I needed him. That night, he packed what he could and came to live with me full time and we intentionally worked to repair our relationship.

Since then, our relationship has never been the same. He's my guy and I'm his hero. He's still independent and sometimes wayward and hardheaded, but he knows he can always depend on dad to see him through anything and everything. When he turned twenty-one, we spent every day of his birthday week together. We made more of those special memories. We went to a spa, had Bible study over lunch at a downtown café, did some financial planning, and set goals for his future. The message I wanted to plant in his heart was that no matter what, we will always have each other. But I also wanted him to get the message that even when he's on his own, things can be better if he chooses better because that power lies within him. He's made me a better father and a better man. Just like the Son of God only did what pleases the Father, my son once told me, "Dad, all I've ever wanted to do was make you proud of me."

In Matthew 3:17 (NIV), God spoke from heaven, "This is my Son, whom I love; with him I am well pleased." I don't know if Joseph ever made a public declaration of his feelings toward Jesus, but that's one thing I don't need Joseph to show me how to do. From the days when my son was a little kid to now, every time we see each other and every time we part ways, he kisses me. At school, at church, at the mall, when it's just us or even when his friends are around. It doesn't matter. It's his way of declaring, "This is my dad and I love him." He may not be Jesus, I may not be God and he may still drive me nuts, but Talorien Marquis Townsend is my son and with him I am well pleased. If you have children, do something today to let them know you love them, support them and believe in them. It will make you a better person in the process.

Chapter 12 - Decisions, Decisions

I blame Adam and Eve. Yup. I blame them for mankind having to work a 9 – 5 job, rent that is too high and cars whose tanks have to be filled up every other day. I blame them for grown kids who live at home and don't work, for red lights when you're in a hurry, for being confused twice a year about when to Fall back or to Spring forward and don't even get me started with understanding leap year. The way I see it, if Adam and Even hadn't started experimenting with grace, our lives would be much easier. I mean they had one rule to follow, don't eat the fruit! But no, Eve got the bright idea to have a picnic with a talking snake and we still don't know where Adam disappeared. But I can imagine now after they've suffered their consequences and have made their peace with God, they are both in heaven looking down on mankind saying, "You all sure have a lot to say about what we did. But look at you!" All of us are faced with situations in life that challenge our better judgment. Although we may not have control over being introduced to compromising situations, we are held accountable for the decisions that we make. Those decisions may lead us down a path of endless possibilities or deliver us to a dark and lonely corner of despair. The path of righteous living is not without temptation and the road of destruction is not without detours that lead to redemption.

FUNNY FAITH

As I was finishing this book my best friend Michelle called me and said that her car would not start. She's the friend who moved to Portland, Oregon that I mentioned in chapter 2. We had plans for her to drive to Seattle so that we could attend a music event. Trying to cheer her up I said, "Well maybe God is protecting you for something on the highway. The weather is pretty bad." Still, that possibility as divine as I tried to make it sound did not stop her from trying to figure out what was wrong with her car. She called back a half hour later explaining that since she didn't want to put 200 additional miles on her car, she had planned to rent a car. She was on her way to the car rental company when her car just stopped completely. After some deductive reasoning she figured out that although her car was in perfect working condition, her gas gauge was not working. She had run out of gas. I started laughing and began to think how that is just like God. So often, God protects us without even exposing us to the possibility of danger. Michelle could have been headed down Interstate 5 and ran out of gas in the dead of night in the middle of nowhere. But God, without speaking through a burning bush or shaking the earth, impressed on her to just rent a car. And in following that unction, He also showed her the peril she had escaped. God makes me laugh sometimes.

No matter which path you are on today, I pray that this book has helped you see that God is always watching over us, always speaking to us and always guiding us. In every phase of our lives and turn of events, He has designed lessons that will forever shape our future and bring understanding and purpose to our past. Pay attention to your life and tell the story for His glory. All we have to do is listen when He speaks, watch when He moves and follow where He leads. Our loving obedience to Him in faith is all He asks of us. Even with our imperfections, it's our *funny faith* that helps us overcome - that's what makes God laugh with joy.

About the Author

Elder Sam Townsend Jr. is probably best known for his distinctive and dramatic ministry style which captivates audiences, compels worshippers and ushers in the Glory of God. He is not only a multi-talented and widely celebrated Choir Master, but an anointed leader, pioneer, trendsetter, ground breaker, prequel and innovator. Aristotle said it best, *"We are what we repeatedly do. Therefore, excellence then is not an act, but a habit."* This quote best describes Elder Townsend who exudes excellence in all of his endeavors. He has served for over 25 years as the Executive Administrator, an ordained elder, Youth Pastor, and Minister of Music at the Greater Glory Ministries Church of God in Christ in Seattle Washington under the pastorate of his father, Superintendent Sam Townsend, Sr. He currently serves as the Minister of Music & Worship Arts and Administrator of the New Beginnings Christian Fellowship in Kent Washington. He has gained a reputation of committed and sacrificial ministry that has earned him great respect and admiration from coast to coast and across all denominational lines.

A father, Author, Worship Leader, Bible Teacher, Preacher and award winning Director, he is also the CEO of two entities through which he trains and empowers the current and next generation of ministry leaders. The *Imani Fellowship Choir* founded in 1996, serves as an evangelistic word and music ministry which has produced some of the greatest singers, song writers, choir directors, recording artists and preachers. Whether in concert or revival, through his uniquely transparent and relevant delivery of the Gospel, countless souls have been impacted, healed, delivered and set free. *The Townsend School of Music & Arts* founded in 2013, provides the foundation for all of his workshops, seminars and music ministry support services designed to address the varied needs of up and coming singers, worship leaders, pastors and churches. He has won numerous awards and recognition not only for his dedication to exemplification of ministry excellence but also for his commitment to the development of other servant leaders.

He has traveled extensively throughout Canada, Europe, Africa and the United States carrying the Gospel, facilitating workshops, performing in concerts, serving as Master of Ceremonies, acting in major stage plays and has shared the stage with music legends such as Dave Hollister, Kim Burrell, Chris Thomlin, the Clark Sisters and BeBe Winans. He has served as the State Minister of Music for the Washington State COGIC Jurisdiction and is currently an Executive Member of the International COGIC Music Department serving as the President of the Northwest Region. He is an instructor for the Applied Studies Institute of the International COGIC Music Department and is also a faculty member of the Academic Division of the James Cleveland Gospel Workshop of America, Inc. He is the Assistant Coordinator of the Quorum of Directors of the International COGIC Music Department and is one of its lead directors under the leadership of the International COGIC Minister of Music, Dr. Judith Christie McAllister. He now adds to his extensive list of accomplishments the publication of his first book *Funny Faith – I'm Convinced God is Somewhere Laughing at Me,* a collection of humors and spiritually infused personal life lessons.

Elder Townsend accepted Christ as his personal savior at the age of seven and spent his formative years and his adulthood dedicated to pursuing God's plan for his life. Today, with over three decades of ministry he stands as a challenger, a changer and a champion with an uncompromising commitment to Christ, the Call and the Kingdom. His ministry transcends race, gender, age, denomination and he is devoted to leading others into a genuine relationship with Christ as well as with each other in the body of Christ.

CPSIA information can be obtained
at www.ICGtesting.com
Printed in the USA
FSOW02n0813291016
26699FS